looking-glass   twinkle, twinkle, little bat   fru

ry   snicker-snack   treacle-well   how doth the little crocodile

urble   twinkle, twinkle, little bat   beamish   phlizz   burb

wling   off with their heads!   manxome   gyre   curiouser

eautiful soup, so rich and green   mimsy   beamish   borogov

ve   slithy   much of a muchness   gimble   twinkle

rabbit-hole   nyctograph   reeling and writing   frabjou

cheshire cat   jubjub   outgrabe   frumious   drawling

! brillig   mimsy   uffish   uglification   mome rath

ormouse say?   portmanteau   snark   tulgey   through the look

treacle-well   un-birthday   callooh! callay!   jabberwocky

ouser and curiouser   gyre   chortle   whiffling   tove

as before breakfast   slithy   jubjub   galumphing   how doth the little

Ye golden hours of Life's young spring,

Of innocence, of love and truth!

Bright, beyond all imagining,

Thou fairy-dream of youth!

I'd give all the wealth that years have piled,

The slow result of Life's decay,

To be once more a little child

For one bright summer-day.

—from "Solitude" by Lewis Carroll

ONE FUN DAY
WITH LEWIS CARROLL

A Celebration of Wordplay
and a Girl Named Alice

WRITTEN BY **Kathleen Krull**

ILLUSTRATED BY **Júlia Sardà**

Houghton Mifflin Harcourt

Boston   New York

LEWIS CARROLL was an expert at fun. A day with Lewis was always fabulous and joyous—as he would say, frabjous.

Young Lewis could make anyone grin from ear to ear, like a Cheshire cat. His ten brothers and sisters adored him. He coaxed them into games of cards, chess, and croquet. He led adventures, galumphing across the leafy wonderland of the English countryside. They found rabbit holes to peer down, toads and caterpillars to befriend, flowers to talk to, trees to climb. Their burbles of delight would brighten the tulgey wood around them.

Best of all, Lewis made up stories and drew pictures. His drawings weren't as
splendid as his tales, but his siblings didn't care. His playfulness with words sent
them all into complete Jabberwocky.

Lewis started writing down his stories and poems. He loved to find new ways to make words play together on a page. "Wow! Wow! Wow!"

Even after he grew into a prim and proper Victorian gentleman, Lewis still loved fun. He didn't want any child feeling mimsy in his company. To amuse the children of his friends, he kept closets full of mechanical toys and dolls. He took the children on trips to the circus or the theater or a Wild West show. He played games, inventing new rules for extra fun, and he encouraged pranks, such as climbing up a clock tower to strike the enormous bell at the wrong time of day.

His young friends never knew what a day with Lewis would hold. Sometimes he'd propose six impossible things before breakfast:

Should they draw ridiculous things, like much of a muchness?

Should they try to soothe the Jubjub bird?

Should they argue with the mysterious twins Tweedledum and Tweedledee?

Should they beware the dreaded Boojum?

Should they go on a hunt for the Snark?

Should they play with a vorpal blade as it goes snicker-snack?

Lewis ran races and gave un-birthday presents. He could even make schoolwork fun. Who knew that one could study Reeling and Writing? That arithmetic included Uglification?

As a fun day turned **brillig**, Lewis hosted picnics under the **Tumtum** tree with tea and cold chicken. He always brought a basket full of yummy cakes, taking care to keep them away from the **toves**.

Anyone who had to miss a fun day out with Lewis Carroll would be **frumious**.

Then came one fine, famous Friday in July, when Lewis began to spin

a story like no other. Rowing a boat with a friend and the three daughters

of another friend, he began telling a tale about a girl named Alice. It was

no coincidence that one of the girls was also named Alice. Perhaps she was

sleepy from the sounds of the oars dipping and the water dripping. Perhaps

she was feeling uffish.

But now she cheered right up.

A girl with her name had just tumbled down a rabbit hole.

Lewis later admitted he had no idea what would happen next. But on the spot, continuing to row, he kept playing with words. In his story, Alice follows a White Rabbit. She finds a bottle that says DRINK ME and a cake that says EAT ME. She keeps growing larger and smaller, sometimes nine feet high, sometimes three inches tall. In this crazy wonderland, all the animals talk, even the caterpillar, and so do the flowers and plants: "We're all mad here."

Oh, this was getting curiouser and curiouser.

A pack of cards plays croquet—using live hedgehogs and flamingos. Sea creatures dance the Lobster Quadrille, while Alice interrupts a Mad Tea Party. Everyone chants silly poems and songs, as when a Mock Turtle croons "Beautiful, beautiful soup!" over and over.

Lewis's friends in the boat were glued to their seats, not daring to gyre or gimble. Not even a Bandersnatch could have distracted them. Lewis added details that kept the real Alice and her sisters beamish, and also peppered the tale with things that would tickle grownups. He threw in breathless escapes, witty arguments about nothing, and one slithy surprise after another.

His brave hero, Alice, copes with it all until the very last minute. Then the pack of cards comes whiffling down upon her——awakening her from her most curious dream.

His friends, rocking in the boat, were wonderstruck. Was there a moral to Lewis's story? No! It was just for fun. Callooh! Callay!

"Write it down!" said the real Alice. She was ten and, like the Queen of Hearts, a bit bossy.

So he did.

Two years after that famous boat ride, Lewis presented the real Alice with a handwritten copy of what became *Alice's Adventures in Wonderland,* with his own illustrations.

When he later published the story as a book, with much better pictures by someone else, readers all over the world erupted in chortles. In no time, Lewis was rich, famous, and busy writing his second book about Alice, this time sending her through the looking glass.

Lewis Carroll, the man who never forgot how to play, had turned a day of fun into stories that were fabulous and joyous—as he would say, frabjous.

Words and Ideas Invented or Adapted by Lewis Carroll

Bandersnatch: An imaginary creature too fast to flee from.

Beamish: Beaming, or radiant with happiness.

Boojum: An especially dangerous Snark (perhaps derived from *bogeyman* or *boo*), so scary that Carroll did not allow it to be illustrated.

Brillig: Late afternoon, related to *broil,* as in broiling food for dinner.

Burble: A mixture of *bleat, murmur,* and *warble.*

Callooh! Callay!: An exclamation of joy, as in "Hurrah! Hooray!"

Cheshire Cat: Unknown origin, perhaps named for the county of Cheshire in the north of England, where Carroll grew up. His version is an imaginary cat that can appear and disappear, leaving its grin behind.

Chortle: A combination of *chuckle* and *snort.*

Curiouser and Curiouser: What Alice says in astonishment as she grows larger and smaller.

Drink Me: When Alice follows these instructions on a bottle she finds, she discovers that the contents taste like cherry tart, pineapple, and hot buttered toast.

Eat Me: Alice finds this spelled out in raisins on a cupcake, and she promptly obeys.

Lobster Quadrille

Tove

Jubjub

FRABJOUS: A combination of *fair, fabulous,* and *joyous.*

FRUMIOUS: A mixture of *fuming* and *furious.*

GALUMPHING: A blend of *galloping* and *triumphant,* meaning an irregular bounding movement.

GIMBLE: To turn around, like a screw being screwed in.

GYRE: To turn around or gyrate, or possibly to scratch like a dog.

JABBERWOCKY: Based on *jabber,* nonsensical speech or, in Carroll's words, "excited and voluble discussion," this was the title of his most famous nonsense poem.

JUBJUB: A moody imaginary bird.

LOBSTER QUADRILLE: A quadrille is a difficult kind of square dance, fashionable during the Victorian era; Carroll's version is performed by turtles, seals, salmon, and lobsters, ending with the lobsters being thrown out to sea: "Will you, won't you, will you, won't you, won't you join the dance?"

MAD TEA PARTY: Famous bizarre gathering of the March Hare, the Mad Hatter, and the Dormouse.

MIMSY: Unhappy, based on *flimsy* and *miserable.*

MOCK TURTLE: Sad creature who sobs as he tells his life story, starting with when he was a real turtle.

MUCH OF A MUCHNESS: An old English expression referring to two or more things having little difference between them—in other words, pretty much the same thing.

Bandersnatch

Snark

Tweedledum and Tweedledee

QUEEN OF HEARTS: The playing-card character who continually shouts "Off with their heads!"

REELING AND WRITHING: A variation on the school subjects of reading and writing.

SIX IMPOSSIBLE THINGS BEFORE BREAKFAST: What the White Queen claims to believe as she urges Alice to believe in the impossible.

SLITHY: Combining *slimy* and *lithe*, described by Carroll as "smooth and active"; possibly related to a word meaning slovenly.

SNARK: An imaginary animal, perhaps combining *snail* and *shark*. Carroll always claimed he had no clear idea what it was.

SNICKER-SNACK: A sound like clicking or snipping.

TOVE: An imaginary type of white badger that lives on cheese.

TULGEY: Dense, dark, and gloomy, though at least once Carroll admitted he didn't really know what the word meant.

TUMTUM: Carroll's name for an imaginary tree, this term would seem to derive from *tumtum*, Victorian slang for the sound of a stringed instrument.

TWEEDLEDUM AND TWEEDLEDEE: Carroll may have been the first to name characters after this expression, which has been around since the 1700s and means "two people resembling each other so closely that they are practically indistinguishable."

UFFISH: Similar to *huffish*, or in a huff; Carroll called it "a state of mind when the voice is gruffish, the manner roughish, and the temper huffish."

UGLIFICATION: According to the Mock Turtle, one of the four branches of arithmetic: Ambition, Distraction, Uglification, and Derision (addition, subtraction, multiplication, and division).

DRINK ME

White Rabbit

Mock Turtle

UN-BIRTHDAY: Any day other than one's birthday, which means everyone has 364 of them.

VORPAL: Keen and deadly, though Carroll later said he had no idea what this word meant.

"WE'RE ALL MAD HERE": What the Cheshire cat says to Alice as a way of explaining Wonderland.

WHIFFLING: Blowing in short puffs.

WHITE RABBIT: The mysterious creature always running ahead of Alice and looking at his watch; one of the most famous rabbits in literature.

"WOW! WOW! WOW!": The chorus of the strange lullaby the peppery Duchess sings to the pig baby in Wonderland.

Nearly two hundred words invented or adapted by Carroll appear in the Oxford English Dictionary, including those in this glossary.

Red: From *Through the Looking-Glass, and What Alice Found There*
Blue: From *The Hunting of the Snark*
Green: From *Alice's Adventures in Wonderland*

Queen of Hearts

Cheshire Cat

More About Lewis Carroll's Journey to the Alice Books

Charles Lutwidge Dodgson (1832-1898) lived in England during the Victorian era. It was a stuffy time, when even children's books weren't intended to be fun: instead, they were to offer lectures about good behavior. His father was a priest in the Church of England, and his mother was busy keeping their huge household running. As the oldest son, Charles became like a third parent to his ten brothers and sisters, a responsibility he shouldered with enthusiasm.

In his twenties, always playing with words, he translated "Charles Lutwidge" into Latin and then back into English, reversing the words to become "Lewis Carroll," the name by which we know him today.

Deeply religious, he became a church deacon and an Oxford professor of math and logic. He was also wildly creative, and "Lewis Carroll" was the name he used for his more whimsical writing. After all, he didn't want to subtract from his reputation as the author of such mathematical tomes as *A Syllabus of Plane Algebraical Geometry: Systematically Arranged, with Formal Definitions, Postulates, and Axioms* (1860).

With such a serious job, as well as the care of his ten siblings all his life, he often felt burdened. It rested his brain to play with the children of his friends. Like many of his favorite writers—Dickens, Tennyson, Blake, Coleridge, Wordsworth—he idealized the innocence of children. "They are three-fourths of my life," he said. "I cannot understand how anyone could be bored by little children."

"He was one of us," one boy said later, "and never a grown-up pretending to be a child."

Carroll couldn't stand the thought of a child being hurt, and he donated large sums to children's hospitals and to charities that helped poor women and children. He never married, but he was an ideal honorary uncle, keeping in touch with young friends by way of thousands of amusing letters.

When he died at age sixty-five, many of his friends sent wreaths to decorate his burial site. They included Alice Liddell Hargreaves, the source of inspiration on that July 4, 1862, boat ride up the River Thames.

Carroll left behind two of the greatest gifts to children ever: *Alice's Adventures in Wonderland* (1865) and *Through the Looking-Glass, and What Alice Found There* (1871). The drawings, by an artist he admired, John Tenniel, were the perfect match.

His were some of the first books ever written for amusement: they have no moral. In time, after the Bible and the works of Shakespeare, they became the books most frequently quoted and translated around the world. They inspired movies, video games, graphic novels, popular songs, theme park rides, operas, and much more.

Lewis Carroll in a self-portrait, 1857

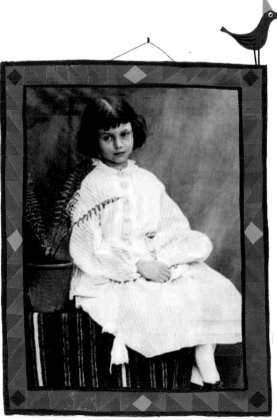

Alice Liddell as photographed by Lewis Carroll, 1860

Sources

Carpenter, Angelica Shirley. *Lewis Carroll: Through the Looking Glass*. Minneapolis: Lerner, 2003.

Carroll, Lewis. *The Humorous Verse of Lewis Carroll*. New York: Dover, 1960.

Cohen, Morton N. *The Letters of Lewis Carroll, Volume One*. New York: Oxford University Press, 1979.

Cohen, Morton N. *Lewis Carroll: A Biography*. New York: Knopf, 1995.

Gardner, Martin, editor, updated by Mark Burstein. *The Annotated Alice: The Definitive Edition*. New York: Norton, 2015.

Green, Roger Lancelyn, editor. *The Diaries of Lewis Carroll, Volume One*. New York: Oxford University Press, 1954.

Woolf, Jenny. *The Mystery of Lewis Carroll: Discovering the Whimsical, Thoughtful, and Sometimes Lonely Man Who Created Alice in Wonderland*. New York: St. Martin's, 2010.

For Melanie Armour, Jana Carlson,
Angelica Shirley Carpenter, and all Alice lovers—K.K.

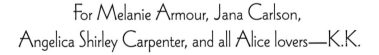

Text copyright © 2018 by Kathleen Krull ◆ Illustrations copyright © 2018 by Júlia Sardà ◆ All rights reserved.

For information about permission to reproduce selections from this book, write to trade.permissions@hmhco.com

or to Permissions, Houghton Mifflin Harcourt Publishing Company, 3 Park Avenue, 19th Floor, New York, New York 10016.

www.hmhco.com ◆ The text type was set in Wade Sans Light Std. ◆ The display type was set in Captain Kidd. ◆ Book design by Opal Roengchai

Library of Congress Cataloging-in-Publication Data ◆ Names: Krull, Kathleen, author. | Sardà, Júlia, illustrator. Title: One fun day with Lewis Carroll :

a celebration of wordplay and a girl named Alice / Kathleen Krull ; Illustrated by Júlia Sardà. Other titles: A celebration of wordplay and a girl named Alice

Description: Boston : Houghton Mifflin Harcourt, [2017] Identifiers: LCCN 2016029373 | ISBN 9780544348233 (hardcover)

Subjects: LCSH: Carroll, Lewis, 1832-1898—Language—Juvenile literature. | Carroll, Lewis, 1832-1898—Juvenile literature. | Plays on words—Juvenile literature.

| Carroll, Lewis, 1832-1898. | Authors, English—19th century—Biography—Juvenile literature. | Children's stories—Authorship—Juvenile literature.

Classification: LCC PR4612 .K78 2017 | DDC 828/.809 [B] —dc23 LC record available at https://lccn.loc.gov/2016029373

Manufactured in China ◆ SCP 10 9 8 7 6 5 4 3 2 1 ◆ 4500675853

3 1886 00228 9556

rtmanteau snark tulgey chortle through

bandersnatch gyre whiffling uffish boojum jabberw

lification six impossible things before breakfast tulgey

tweedledum and tweedledee jabberwocky burble d

rillig oh my ears and whiskers! curiouser and curiouser

through the looking-glass vorpal galumphing boro

un-birthday callooh! callay! jubjub brillig down

nyctograph much of a muchness vorpal frabjous snar

uglification borogove cheshire cat oh my ears and whis

how doth the little crocodile jabberwocky gyre but what did th

six impossible things before breakfast snark snicker-snack beami

gimble tove phlizz mischmasch bandersnatch cu

eautiful soup so rich and green much of a muchness six impossible